Eulogy for a Private Man

Eulogy for a Private Man

Fred Dings

 TRIQUARTERLY BOOKS
NORTHWESTERN UNIVERSITY PRESS
Evanston, Illinois

TriQuarterly Books
Northwestern University Press
Evanston, Illinois 60208-4210

Printed in the United States of America

ISBN 0-8101-5093-X (cloth)
ISBN 0-8101-5094-8 (paper)

The paper used in this publication meets the minimum requirements of the American
National Standard for Information Sciences—Permanence of Paper for Printed
Library Materials, ANSI Z39.48-1984.

For Maria

Downward to darkness, on extended wings

Contents

Part Two

Part Three

Acknowledgments

The poems collected in this volume previously appeared in the following publications:

High Plains Literary Review, "Dissertation on Dogs," "Planes," "Transitory Music."

Paris Review, "Sunday Evening" (as "The Evening After"), "Dido."

Poet Lore, "In the Season of Memory."

Poetry, "Chains of Change," "The Fire," "Letter to Genetically Engineered Superhumans," "The Man and the Cemetery Effigy," "Migratory Flight," "The Past," "Revelations," "Words for a Perfect Evening."

Quarterly West, "To My Tongue."

TriQuarterly, "The Bodily Beautiful," "Claims of the Past," "Eulogy for a Private Man," "Two Sketches of Solitude," "The Unlived," "Woman with Gravitas."

Western Humanities Review, "The Glowing Coal," "The Last Voyage."

PART ONE

Words for a Perfect Evening

Even a perfect evening eventually yawns
and goes to sleep to awaken changed in the morning.
Each day must be wrestled for beauty among

this permanent impermanence where clouds shift their shape
in the shifting wind and the sudden blossomings of illness,
the carcinomas in the brain, change the possible

future to a river's mouth widening at the sea's edge.
And yet there is a durability here,
lives that somehow replenish themselves

around a center in the gravity of affection, the way
the earth turns itself to be touched everywhere
by the light. What else can I say to you tonight,

that meaning is the wine we press from the context we share,
that our daily devotion depends on a presence and absence,
on arms that gather the invisible flowers we find

growing among our ruins, and arms that bear
nothing but a guarded emptiness, a space preserved,
a dependable harbor waiting for someone we love.

The Fire

When I was a child, the elderly frightened me.
They were the withered ones near death. Their faces
shriveled around their skulls like prunes on pits.

All the rivers of the world had gouged their skin,
and their spidery legs were webbed with bruised veins.
Once, a woman's watering eyes glared

at me with pools of fire, and I saw myself
reflected there like a fly stuck in that burning.
But now, my body's singing stutters in pain,

and the waterways of time sculpt my face.
The web tightens its net. The future shrinks,
but each moment swells with a fullness of past

I never could have guessed. I imagine an end
so sated with life that I drop out of time
like ripe fruit to the earth. I imagine

a moment so wide that I spread from my body
and embrace everything like the sky.
But lullabies are easy in times of peace,

and lately I search the eyes of the old for the white
burn of a mind defying the body's betrayals,
for a humor and kindness free among the ruins,

for a glimpse of spirit beneath the flesh that sloughs
like velvet on antlers, a spirit *almost visible,*
chiseled with pain, tempered in the fire of this world.

Revelations

Nostalgia for the future beyond
the black wall eclipsed his path.
The earth grew heavy within him and wanted

to sleep. The days no longer buttoned
inside the uniforms of order.
The streams of desire ran dry in their beds.

The light could see no point in staying.
Others around him were looting their lives,
minting children, painting self-portraits

for the coffers of art, or carving sepulchres
of fame to lie in memory forever.
The cairns of despair were everywhere.

Elegies filled the air. But then
he thought how little we live our lives,
how the black wall was a black angel

pointing us back to the moment we have,

to the one grain in the eye of the hourglass,
to the one altar of sacrifice,
to even the moment the heart must fist

to existence and hammer the point of being
like a nail, to even the moment so painful
the mind wants to leap from its fire,

to even the blue cold moment
in caterpillar days that crawl
through the long winters—all must be lived

so endurance can bear its revelation,
and the fist ease to an open palm,
and the fire quench in a time of water,

and the blue turn as rose as the blue
newborn that gasps its first breath
and its two lungs billow like sails.

.

In the Season of Memory

Still, we have this fear of coming to nothing,
of clutching the years at the end like a cluster of stalks,
the long dry flowerless stems of thought,
the deeds leading to dead-end alleys,
leaving not one star-point of meaning
to shine above our sleep in someone's night.

For a brief season of memory our name may be
a berry of sadness sweet on a tongue that speaks it,
a rinse of rain clearing an ear that hears it,
but will there still be time, even at the end,
for some essential drop of mind to spread
like dye momentarily through the clarity of time
or burst like a bubble on a rain-pummeled pond
with some brief scent of individual air?

If only we could be like the stars when they die,
their final explosions of light like death-blossoms
seeding new matter in the fertile night.

Sunday Evening

I.

"Death is also the *thief* of beauty," he says,
as a slow disquietude replaces morning's calm.
The pink light fades from ashen clouds,
and an icy luminosity begins to wax
above the highlands of eternity.
The willow, weeping all evening over rocks
beside the pond, darkens to an arch hunched
above a wafer of sacramental light,
a fallen moon too faint to give much sight.
There were minds which might have ripened into suns
had not the body failed, the nursing vine
sallowed and withered before the fruit was ripe.
We are flowers of light in a field of darkness,
brief in our pulse of generations. We open
and close, wax and wane, open and close.

II.

Death of the body is not the only death.
Our seasons of loss prepare us for the end,
the gardens withered in droughts of circumstance,
the taut and cold receding lips of love,
the glance that lowers and turns away forever,
the fires of hope snuffed by the winds of change
on the ledges above, the dim glitter of stars
in the pond's eye like distant citadels
we'll never know but we had once lived by.
Death of the body is not the only death.
A winter mind that never turns to spring
has had too much of suffering. Its crystal eyes

no longer see the colors of our lives.
An empty house collapses under snow
in whiteness cleansed of feeling long ago.

III.

Where are the stars of death in the pointed night?
Is it sacrilege or only emulation
to want to be a god? A brazen boy
flings against the Goliaths of circumstance,
his sling, a frayed genetic rope he weaves
to the furthest nebulae at the end of thought,
a human tree whose height might reach eternity.
The fire-feathered bird among its branches
sings a human song on the edge of space.
It beckons through the rocks of time and place.
It sings of fire and ice, but not of death.
It sings of seasons and dreams, but not of death.
An ancient king who lingers on his throne
hears its song and dreams of wanderings,
of odysseys among the distant stars.

The Force of Intent

At times we force our destiny like rivers
carving canyons to the sea or trees
that crack the rocks they wedge to reach the light.

But the politics of will depend on change,
the force of our intent in *circumstance.*
How easily we trample the green havens,

dissolve chapels of mist in scorching light.
How quickly we bridle at roadblocks and chasms
and turn from the philosophy of lakes.

But our certainties are destined for revision
like morning maps of an evening land. We know
at last the mountains are more than we supposed,

and our wagons sit stranded by snow in the pass.
The yellow pride of noon turns blue at dusk.
The walking boy becomes the wheelchair man.

The Man and the Cemetery Effigy

The years of failure had wounded his hope beyond
recovery. The erotic postures of possible futures
no longer duped him. His path closed.

Each evening he watched the drape of light
dissolve as night disrobed. At noon he knew
the nakedness of darkness. He stood on the ice of time

waiting to fall through. Then one night
he wandered like a homeless drunk in the cemetery
among the black flames of the trees, the whispering

leaves, the moonlit stones in rows like teeth
with nothing but the sky to bite against,
and there he found the black angel spreading

its wings of despair like a wall eclipsing the stars,
and he knelt in nausea to receive its benediction
and was told to find his freedom in hopelessness,

to find his dignity in obscurity, and to root
his life among the dead where even those
who would be gods eventually grow human.

Words

I do not speak of certain things.
All talk would be the scuffed air

we shovel over the dead. Sometimes
the air is a grave on which no words

will tread, and language stands speechless
on the edge, vivid with silence.

But sometimes words are the only hands
we have to touch a bruised memory

or cleanse a wound that never healed
or lift a body we've carried for years

at last to the pyre of shared grief.
I remember a dying girl, lying

curled in dust, flies on her lips
and eyes, her swollen belly pregnant

with death. I remember her soft, struggling
breath and the hum of flies in the quiet heat.

Letter to a Friend

Who knows what age will bring besides your death?
You think you see your future plod before you,
eventless, a blunt-toothed cog of certainty,

churning for years of noon in summer heat,
but haven't there been times when suddenly you saw
something which had been there all along

and nothing had changed but you, a certain slant
of age, perhaps, or disposition of the eyes,
some newfound sensitivity, awakened when

adversity scraped the skin of your perception?
The starving leaves now blaze with colors
not seen until articulated by the frost.

These years of erosion may yet uncover forgotten
ruins—your own, standing there like a child,
holding out the key to your next room.

Claims of the Past

What if we could find a way to sift
the winds for drifting minds to place in bodies
again? Whom would we choose and why? The saviors

and philosopher kings to stop our squabbling? the poor
who choked in obscurity and filth? the nameless
heroes who sacrificed themselves? the murdered,

the stifled, the unfulfilled? the evil to repair
their shame? the children who barely had a chance?
Who, among all the unredeemed

billions swirling like leaves to be reborn,
wouldn't have some claim for living more?
Isn't it better the dead come back as they do,

briefly, when they surface in a stranger's face
or voice or in a scrap of song, or steadily,
when light shafts through a window in an empty room

and the motes of dust almost coalesce,
or suddenly, when memories storm our solitude
in vacant lots or crowds, clouding us

in pain or refreshing us in a rinse of remembrance,
leaving everything shining, veneered with past,
and perhaps valued more because it does not last.

The Past

The "nameless unremembered acts of kindness"
are never lost. They whisper to our dreams

like a mother's hum on the distant edge of sleep.
They are the ghosts of benevolence whose many

unseen hands lift us in seasons of pain
and lead us to chapels of faith in the stained glass

of our perceptions. Their influence is always there,
the way the stars are always there, even

in day, the distant suns of times past
mixing their light with the bright noon of the present.

The Gift

When we arrive bodiless with only our memories,
will we have loved life enough to paint
its face in light on the black page of eternity?

When our bodies are torn open like envelopes,
what news will our ancestors be able to read in us?
Will we have gathered just a little more

than they, be able to offer some nuance of feeling
or subtlety of perception they had missed,
or at least bear a glow to nurse their nostalgia

and lighten their darkening? Or will we have lived
in vain and fail even to reach the past
which waits ahead gravely with open arms,

fail even to recognize their faces
which then will turn from us, stranding us
like feeble stars in the dark space of ignorance?

The Glowing Coal

As he had feared, the world was going to end
sooner than expected. The future now
narrowed to months. He stepped outside.

A haze had lifted he had not known was there.
Edges of things seemed sharp enough to cut.
The world glittered. He stood inside a diamond.

So much had been held back, so much to spend.
He felt a sudden love for everything,
even the moldering garbage at his feet.

Each swirl and eddy of the world, each smell,
flavor, hue, touch, and tone would now
burn inside the flame of his attention.

He would not lapse, even inside his pain.
If only this coal he carried to the darkness
would somehow take eternity to fade.

Transitory Music

Each Sunday he'd go with his family
up the stony lane to the church,
its gray stones mortared tight,
its windows plain as daylight,
its one steeple like a blunt thorn
scratching cries from the invisible wind.
They'd all be there: the bored deadbeats,
the sleepy obligated children,
the worn seeking peace, the mournful
and frightened laying their pain on the altar
of belief, the cheery pews of hopefuls
planting themselves in rows like bulbs,
the reverent who had almost grown mute.

Some days he'd almost join the leafless
trees in pleading with the sky,
but he knew he would squander eternity,
having only lived a few
moments of his life. A moment
fully lived, he thought, would be like air
embracing everything that is.
He kept breathing past redemption,
though sometimes he heard a music
scratched into being by the thorns of experience
and stood inside the stained light
and felt the rose open, the fist
unclench its five fingers of sense,
and he carried an open hand
for as long as he could into the world.

The Unlived

If only he could memorize like a lover
the body of the ordinary, which was already
a dream much larger than all sleep.

He regretted the future—the one he *would* have lived—
the way he regretted the past, the fossil record
of mere fact, the life that died into being

while all the unlived possibilities
echoed into silence among the vaulted
arches and stained-glass rosettes of time.

Each day was proof of his failure to flare
into ash at the flashpoint of recognition
or crack ecstatically open in the globed moment,

saving nothing for his next breath. How easily
his imagination yawned and slept, how vision
grew young and frolicked in the shallows of perception.

His mind floated like a sponge in an ocean, soaked
full by a mere palmful of water, immersed
in all that it would never come to know.

Planes

The season of heat had passed.
Rain had deepened the dust
with umber and raw sienna.

Houses had gathered inward
there on the treeless hill.
He heard two voices pass

and the clopple of horses on cobbles
fade out of reach. The street
began to fill with mist,

which drifted from the valley below
as if searching for something . . . a way
to give itself a shape,

some form among the forms.
It drifted from house to house,
pressing its wet face

against the nearly invisible
planes of the windowpanes,
baffled it could not go

where it could see—places
he would never be
and never know why.

There was something about
the matter of his domain,
the density of his life.

At the Grand Canyon

Clouds float like islands in the river of air
which flows between the walls. The Colorado,

a sliver of water, glints at the bottom like a knife.
Ephemeral as fruit flies, airplanes flit

among the cliffs, while laden mules labor
down to a present millions of years below.

On the edge of the gouge, herds of awed tourists
gape at the immense ruined rainbows of time.

"I wish we could live here," someone says,
not noticing the clutch of desert plants

struggling at his feet, which soon will die
and blow across the stones, stain the rocks,

or lodge as molecules of dust in someone's eye.
How much grandeur does it take until

our eyes fall to the small life before us,
the geologic blink we call our lives,

how long before we settle on a few roots
finding life in a handful of burning sand,

keeping their grip inside the wind which whistles
faintly as it whets against their limbs?

PART TWO

Letter to Genetically Engineered Superhumans

You are the children of our fantasies of form,
our wish to carve a larger cave of light,
our dream to perfect the ladder of genes and climb

its rungs to the height of human possibility,
to a stellar efflorescence beyond all injury
and disease, with minds as bright as newborn suns

and bodies which leave our breathless mirrors stunned.
Forgive us if we failed to imagine your loneliness
in the midst of all that ordinary excellence,

if we failed to understand how much harder
it would be to build the bridge of love
between such splendid selves, to find the path

of humility among the labyrinth of your abilities,
to be refreshed without forgetfulness,
and weave community without the threads of need.

Forgive us if you must reinvent our flaws
because we failed to guess the simple fact
that the best lives must be less than perfect.

The Bodily Beautiful

Ah, the bodily beautiful, how they are envied
for the perfect rhymes of their bodies' moons and stars,
how the world sets sail for the labial latitudes
of their lustrous skin, forgetting the bloody factories

within. But what of their burden, the daily swelter
in the spotlights of lust, the lovesick legions
and crush of attentive puppets, the ceaseless chatter
and charades of mating games, the splatter of night-

frightened moths who fling against their panes?
How hard it must be among fiestas
of permission and satin pillows to practice forbearance
and cleanse the spirit in the deserts of self-denial,

how hard to leave the shallows of sexuality
and immerse in the treacherous waters of love, to glimpse
the skull of time in the mirror's lie and the bones
of honesty inside those sublime impediments of flesh.

The Woman with Gravitas

There's nothing now she wants or needs from us.
A sad and liquid peace has filled her eyes.

The wreckage of her life has massed inside her,
the way the dust of stars now forms the earth.

The weight of her despair outweighs the world,
so all things bend or fall towards her center.

Children climb into the safety of her arms.
Men and women orbit her like moons.

She seldom speaks, but smiles and listens patiently.
She moves inside a weather of her own

like an evening star which seems to grow more bright
the more it grows immersed inside the night.

Eulogy for a Private Man

He would not arrange his face to please us,
smile on cue or chime with ritual greeting,
would not distill himself into an aperitif,

dance or fence or wrestle with clever speech,
add to the litter of words that silence sweeps.
He was a dry stream, flowing unseen beneath

his arid bed, a social counterweight
to the harlequins of humid revelation.
But sometimes a lean, muscular sentence would stride

before us and cross its arms in a stubborn stance,
then turn away, as if remembering how the flimsy
bridges we fling to span the abyss collapse,

how our strings of meaning unravel as we speak.
He annoyed us and intrigued us, a hieroglyph
of cliff-faced solitude we tried to decipher.

But perhaps such a stern gravity was necessary
to keep his secret wild moons circling,
or perhaps he preferred the untrammeled woods

of his loneliness and reserved it as a private garden
for one who never came, or perhaps some eclipse
of love produced an arctic cold, a sentinel

trusting no one at the gate, or perhaps
he kept a monstrous rage inside his torment
which could not lapse for one mauled moment.

Who knows the terms of another's life? For some
it may be a victory even to achieve
a distant closeness, an intimate alienation.

In the Humid Zone

No doubt we should garden our emotions,
pull the weeds of misanthropy, build the bridges
of affection and understanding where we can,

prod ourselves to leave our comfort zones
and our gazing through the windowpanes of books.
No doubt we should find our way outside

among the grid of streets and scabs of concrete,
among the herds of humid personalities,
the brushfires of contention, the abrasive crudity,

the social pirates, the webs of intrigue,
the conquerors who try to colonize our minds,
the sledgehammers and foghorns of opinion

whose statements drop to the floor and gather flies,
the cloying hormones, the drones of mincing minds.
No doubt we should suffer this swelter

if only to be reminded of our unperfected
patience, our small forgiveness, the great growth
still required of our insufficient love.

The Family Gatherings

For years they could barely attend. Rivalries smoked
with resentment. Fuses ignited with a nuance or glance.
They postured, arms crossed, and read their lines

from ghost scripts and the private agendas of pride.
They railroaded each other with filial ties,
wrapped with presumption, and fettered with obligation.

But in time they felt a sadness drift
into their midst, a disappointment with the deaf
world. An hourglass turned in their bodies,

and the old issues stopped smoldering. The air
cleared in the amber light of middle age.
They found a common gravity in the heaviness,

a solace in the vestibule of birth around
the old sun and seed-point of being.
And on those brief afternoons and evenings,

they came bearing the scars of the first severance
to gather back light from a shared past,
to warm themselves at the fire of earthly belonging,

knowing that soon, one by one, they would leave,
and the last would be left with nothing but space to embrace,
the last harvest, an aftermath of air.

Two Sketches of Solitude

A Young Man by the Sea

The pulsing surf spreads its scallops
of foaming lather around the young
man's feet and sucks the silken
sand between his toes. Throbbing
breakers claw and souse the cliff
while lean white wings hover
low and knife against the wind.
Tangles of kelp clump in knots,
and the necklace of shells and bones he kicks
clatter like dice. Polished logs
choke the beach like crossed legs,
and he snuffs the pungent brine and thinks
of swimming out among the rock
stacks wrapped in shawls of mist
thrusting through the waves. Clouds
strew their flaring pastel hues
like lingerie tossed across the sky.
The moon, a molten pearl, laves
the undulant dunes with emollient light,
while grasses comb backwards in the breeze
and whisper from seclusions in the night.

An Old Man by the Sea

The collapsing surf gasps and fans its milky
spittle around the old man's legs
and shifts the sodden sand beneath his feet.
Breakers gnaw at the cliff's battered face
while he treads the wrackline, threading among debris

and stitching a seam which erases in the brine.
Around him shrieking gulls scavenge the bier
of sand, pecking at shards of crabs and clams
among tangled and gangrenous sinews of kelp.
Sun-bleached trees, like bones disgorged
from the maws of storms, lie stranded on the beach.
The stench of eons bleeds into the air
from wind-guttered clumps of feathers and fish,
and the eroded land's last stubborn hunches
stand like gravestones in the scything sea,
encircled sentinels cloaked in mantles of mist.
Among the broken edges of the ashen clouds,
the moon's shell rises like the ghost of the sun,
while lapping waves lull and drone beneath,
beside the unkempt cemetery mounds of sand
and the hollow stalks that clatter in the wind.

Scherzo

Dissertation on Dogs

Your basic dog, you see, is your basic animal.
Untrained, it seems a comical and vulgar creature,
a kind of raging id which lacks all continence.

It pushes through the world teeth first
like a machine whose mission is solely eating meat.
It masticates manure and licks itself in public!

Its tongue hangs and pants and drools, and its nose
is wantonly wet for every pollen of scent.
In short, it's a wonder dogs are commonly sought as pets.

Yet, there are many things to recommend them.
We share a kinship with the dog, expressed
in certain phrases such as "I'm howlin' for you

darlin'" or "I'm hot on the trail of *love*,"
and on dog days in this dog-eat-dog world,
when the warp and woof of our companionship

grows thin, we find a certain friend in the dog,
a kind of caninical law of unswerving loyalty.
We find a fluency in those sympathetic eyes,

the sorrowful stares, the brow-lifts of concern,
and in the tail, a barometer of anger and fear,
a metronome of pleasure thumping on the floor,

and in the voice, a whimper or staccato of pain,
the hatchet blows of obsession, the sirens of yearning,
a forlorn and arctic loneliness to match our own.

In fact, in the presence of such spirituality,
we may wonder if a dog-*soul* exists or merely
an epiphenomenon of canine-mind, a flower

of spirit which wilts when the root of flesh is cut.
This question further taunts us when we note
a comportment of restraint in an *old* dog, an economy

of wag, an air of wisdom in the graying at the eyes,
and a meditative posture readily assumed
when the nose rests on paws in an attitude of prayer.

In summation, I leave you with this question:

could they be some higher form, visiting disguised,
say lovable angels who lower themselves to train us
in the purity, fidelity, and art of adoration?

Expeditions of a Misanthrope

Whenever he safaried to the jungle swirl,
the gadflies goaded. The vines of alliance curled

their tendrils of obligation around his limbs.
The piranhas, schooled, waited for him to swim.

The parrots chattered. The snakes slithered in pits.
The monkeys grabbed each other's tails and pinched.

The wolves and vultures circled mating pairs.
The macaws displayed their scarlet feathers for a fare.

The lions and hyenas mawled the bleating meek.
The rats crawled in fecal mass and reeked.

He always left, wondering why he came
so unpracticed and unwilling to play in jungle games.

To My Tongue

Slug of mud.
Sloth slumped among the white stumps.
How you slumber through your nights! Don't
you know you'll have eternity to rot?
True, you need your due of rest,
but then you waste your wakefulness!
Gullet's doorstep, foraging food-slave,
think what life you drag each day to your altar
just to sate the taste-gods warting on your back,
and think then of that other taste, O chef d'amour,
how you sponge the feverish lips of your mate
then twist in the garden like two snakes.
But all this daily fare could be forgiven
if, as chef d'air, you weren't such a cheap magician,
performing the same stale tricks and nervous tics.
O chameleon of shape, you heave and sink,
scuff and stipulate the air, but fail to think.
Your blather just ensnares and lathers the obvious.
You wag with praise,
bite with spite,
smoke with subterfuge and guile,
and this meaninglessness you call your life.

I should lock you in your room,
robed in monastic gloom and silence.
How else but as a scholar of despair
will you someday learn to pare your words
to dredge the shallows and unclench a fisted soul,
whisper solace to the grieving who crack with ache,

or incense your prayer with aftertaste for God.
What but darkness can teach a clod to speak with light?

I know, I know. You are not to blame.
I am the hearse of thought. You are only the valet.

Prufrock Meets a Colleague

"How are you?" he asks again today.
What if I were to make a stand and speak
and act only in ways consistent with
my feelings? Do I dare? Do I dare
not smile on cue, erupt with automatic
greeting and lose myself again among
the same synaptic forests of response?
I should close the factory, tear the chafing
collar, kick away these pinching shoes—
after all, so many others do.
You see them on the evening news with signs,
blaring demands, refusing civil law . . .
but then, there are so many warring factions.
It's clear the boundaries of our states of mind
require some concession to formality,
though I'm tired of inanities and guile.
"Fine," I say again today and pass.
They also serve who only cough and smile.

PART THREE

The Carousel

What if the life force grew tired
of living, tired of the endless invention of forms,

the balloons of meaning, the soufflés of passion, the blather,
the whole lathered carousel of being?

What if the storyteller grew bored of stories,
and the forms of life fell in a twisted scrawl

like graffiti on a rock, and the dust stopped dancing,
and the songs stopped chewing on other songs

to feed their singing, and the poems fell out of sound,
and the stars stopped boiling, and the last wave

of substance flopped on the shore of nonexistence?
Then what would it matter? Who could possibly care?

In the Absence of Rain

Here our sacred ground is cracked with drought.
Poverty whispers like a saw. Clouds pass
as if this rift of dust did not exist.
Our poems call down the rain, but the measured

furrows wait. Our philosophies of pain
are the thin music we drape over silence.
Each day the ruse of possibility
is harder to maintain. The years deepen

the unread lines in the cliff's face. Shall
we mutter restlessly among the white hills
or sit listless in the fields, deformed
by necessity, like the wind-blasted pines

whose branches all trail on one side?
Or shall we give one great sigh,
one great lapse of flesh, and leave
our petitionless bones lying on the miserly earth?

Chains of Change

In drought the mind clouds with humid visions,
and in cold seas we sail for the islands of summer
where pink roses of pleasure petal open

and fall in fleshy halos on the grass. Serenity
waits for us in the green silence after
love, in the aftertaste of wine, in the heaven

where we imagine we could linger forever.
But desire gathers on the boundaries of difference
like droplets on a cold glass in warm air,

and when the sparkling moment eventually warms
to the general mood, the dew steams back
to its former self, drifting toward some

new island in time. Aren't we like that?
Wouldn't the long incarcerations in happiness
leave us longing for sadness, praying for a few

flames to singe our ease, for archipelagos
of pain to erupt in our seas of content as reasons
for sailing, as the indispensable linkage of our lives.

Migratory Flight

We could deny our winters, refuse to cut
our hands mining the sharp ores of grief.
Whenever the cold comes, we could follow

the arrowheads of geese shafting south
to an azure place where whales sing offshore
and otters frolic in the wanton surf.

We could grow soft as children in the arms
of leisure, but we might never learn in time
how to stoke the cold fire of the will

in that winter we cannot refuse, when we must glean
from the icy fields the last scattered grains
we once disdained, with only the luminous pallor

of the moon scarfed in clouds to light our way,
rising above the outstretched arms of the trees
in its long slow journey through the night.

Dido

When he left to plow the sea and husband
other lands, she became all fire.
Her frenzied flames clutched at air. Smoke

coiled over the city and frayed among
the clouds and seaward wind. Her soul weighed
on the pyre and plunged beneath the embers,

thrusting deep into the dark like a root
to the waters of misery. She wandered in woods,
in wastelands and night, robed in the fire

of new arrivals. Others who had darkened
inside their cloaks withdrew from her
like ships among the trees. Her form glared

through the woods. Her stares scorched all
they tried to hold. The littering leaves
burned beneath her feet. She sought the nets

of branches, but none could hold her close enough.
She could not find the swamp to douse herself
inside its pools or find the river to drown

herself inside its embrace. So she wandered,
a fire wrapped in fire. Once, *he* came,
pleading, armored, but she had considered

the nature of ships, the loading and unloading,
the angling of sails for wind, considered
the nature of harbors, open for whatever

sea-weary fates come sailing in.
And so, her ears were closed when he spoke
as if from underwater on the sea's bed.

She choked her words before they could be born,
then clenched inside her fire and wrenched away.
But after that turning inward, she changed.

At first, desire dulling to despair, she started
to darken like the rest, but then no longer
wandered the woods: she stood among the trees,

discerning the shades of shade, the way
loneliness shifted into solitude.
Her glances lingered with understanding,

which frightened many at first, and tremors of speech
rumbled through the silence in that region.
She lightened as the heavy blood of self

drained from her fire, and saffron dawn
welled from the fissure in her chest, spreading
across her soul. She smiled, listening to those

who came to her, consoling them as they took
her light. A glow lingered wherever
she walked. The fragrance of her compassion

incensed the dark. Faces emerged from cowls
and shone, reflecting her affection. Legions
gathered, illumined, a pale and fallen heaven.

There was talk of eviction and further punishment.
The Light and Dark sparked in correspondence.
But in the end, Hell decided it wanted her there

to feed the flames of the damned. Her kindness
would fester as their greatest points of pain,
the seeds of heaven they could never gain.

And Heaven too required that she stay
to show all souls how miracles grow from misery
like roses growing from a bed of coals.

The Rehearsal

Somewhere else there is someone who will never
die. Somewhere else the moonlight washes
the bodies of lovers with milk, nursing their dreams.

Here, the windows suffocate in drapes.
Shadows frieze on the wall. I lie in the heat,
unable to close my eyes, rehearsing myself

for the end, knowing my slot in time will soon
clot with darkness and the last dirt will drum
on my box of borrowed earth. I rehearse

for the time I will choke in a world of air and claw
like a swimmer sinking to the sea's floor. How
will I compose myself, what song will I

have practiced enough to quiet the terrors of hell?
I search the expensive years for a secret rain,
a white noise, a curtain of inner light

I can draw around myself like a shroud.
I walk back through the years, searching
the layers of golden light and dried blood,

all the way back to the black door
before birth where I practice stepping through,
knowing this time it is only a beginning.

The Last Voyage

On nights like this, how clear
the moonlight is, anointing trees
hushed by the water's edge with light
floating on the surface of their leaves.

I think of Crane at the end, slipping
into the dark sea, abandoning everybody,
all bridges down but one,
swimming towards Belle Isle,

his own unbetrayable reply.
Was it like that those last moments
when he grew tired of correspondences
and the flagless piracy of critics, thinking

no deeds but words, no words but deeds,
fulfilling his own prophecy?
I imagine it differently.
This time he floats, a splintered seer,

in the cool Caribbean brine, refusing
the lifesavers tossed to him
like so many hands reaching
into his solitude. This time

the passengers crowd the rail and stare
in disbelief as he, rising
and swelling, watches them crate away,
their bright lights shrinking from sight—

a glowing egg, then a star, then night.
Not all endings are a failure
of the imagination to go on.
There is a sea change of heart

in the dark waters of this version,
a sudden liberation wanting at the last
what maybe was wanted from the start—
not transport, but immersion.

Notes

"Words for a Perfect Evening" is for Maria.

"The Fire" is for Anna Mary Dings.

"Revelations" is for Robin Fisher.

"The Force of Intent" is for John Ashbery.

"The Man and the Cemetery Effigy": Iowa City, Iowa. This poem is for Michael Steinberg.

"Letter to a Friend" is for Michael Dings.

"The Past": The quotation is from William Wordsworth. This poem is for Wilma Kneisley with profound gratitude.

"The Gift" is for Richard Howard.

"Transitory Music" is for Pam Hoover.

"Letter to Genetically Engineered Superhumans" is for Jean Bethke Elshtain.

"The Woman with Gravitas" is for Susan Hahn.

"Eulogy for a Private Man" is for John Robert Eshbach.

"The Family Gatherings" is for Judy Phipps.

"Dissertation on Dogs" is for Ginger, Brownie, Sable, Shawn.

"Prufrock Meets a Colleague": With apologies to Eliot and Milton.

"Migratory Flight" is for Christopher Buckley.

"Dido" is for Mark Strand.

"The Rehearsal" is for Roger Steinberg.

"The Last Voyage" is for Laura Iglar.